HAZEL EVANS
SMALL SPACE GARDENING

HAMLYN

Produced by New Leaf Productions

Photography by Mick Duff
Design by Jim Wire
Typeset by System Graphics
Series Editor: Elizabeth Gibson

First published in 1985 by
Hamlyn Publishing
Bridge House, 69 London Road
Twickenham, Middlesex, England

ISBN 0 600 30646 1

Printed in Spain

Larsa D. L. TF. 731 – 1985

We would like to thank:
Frances McCormack, Jackie Grant, Andrew Green,
Colin Dale and George Rose of Notcutts Garden Centre,
Maidstone, Kent.
Also
Mrs Johanna Vinten, Colin Smith, Marion Dunn, Mr and
Mrs P. Wood and Sheldwich Nurseries, Faversham, Kent.

CONTENTS

INTRODUCTION

It's surprising what you can do with a small space, given a good helping of enthusiasm and a little imagination to go with it. In many ways the more unpromising your surrounds are, the more you have to work at it and—therefore—the more you are encouraged to do something spectacular.

To make up for their lack of elbow-room, many patios and back yards have particular advantages that larger gardens don't necessarily offer. If they are sited in a city, for instance, the micro-climate is almost certainly warmer than in the countryside around; thus you may well find you can experiment with tender plants that might otherwise not survive a sharp winter. Many small space gardens are also set among other buildings so that you get the advantage of high walls against which growing climbers add an extra dimension of greenery.

Having only a small area to work with, you are talking, too, in terms of less outlay, so you can afford to use more exotic materials—real stone paving, perhaps, instead of concrete. You may also be able to afford a few exotic plants. It is important, however, to choose your plants carefully, for everything in a small space garden has to work harder for its living; you can't afford to carry "passengers"; plants that have a brief season when they are at their best but are a liability during the rest of the year. Instead look out for those that will do the double duty of providing attractive flowers or berries *as well as* greenery or an interesting shape.

Planning Hints

Be sure to plan your patio on an all-year-round basis, too, for although you may not actually want to sit out in it during the colder months, it is still more pleasant to be able to look out on a green scene than on walls and concrete. This means taking care to choose a good backdrop of evergreen plants and shrubs to give freshness through the year. You can then top up with colour as you want, changing the scheme from one year to another if you use bedding plants.

With a small plot to plan, it's a good idea to bring in a note of fantasy and fun. You can get away with all sorts of tricks and illusions that simply would not work in a larger space. Mirrors hidden behind wrought iron grilles, for instance, give the illusion of windows in the wall. Or even consider fixing a real door permanently in place to hint that there is a garden beyond. One successful door that I saw had been mounted so it appeared to be just ajar—even more effective. Trellis, too, can be used in all sorts of interesting ways: as a fake arch, for instance, on which to fix real climbers. Paint the centre in a solid dark colour to make the illusion even more successful.

Be sure to make space for living out of doors; even the tiniest roof patio or balcony usually affords space for a chair or a stool or—at the least—a large cushion on which to sit. And if there is room to eat out of doors, too, then you can really go to town. A barbecue need only be a small table-top hibachi, but if you can find room to build one into the side of the patio, better still.

Living out of doors means that you ought to plan for some lighting—an important aspect of patio gardening that is often overlooked. Provided you buy purpose-made equipment (*never* attempt to use indoor cables and fittings; it is extremely dangerous), it is simple to install and does wonders to the decor out of doors. Ideally you should plan for one or two spotlights or floods dotted among your plants; choose the kind mounted on spikes that push into the soil so that you can move them around from one pot or raised bed to another, according to your mood. Permanent lighting (see page 46) plays another important role, too, as a burglar deterrent; a floodlit courtyard is much more daunting to cross than one that is in darkness. Even if permanent lighting is impossible for you, consider using flares mounted on sticks, or candles for special occasions. A small space garden that is lit up at night becomes an enchanting stage set, even if all that is spotlighted is green foliage.

Plan your patio with a unified look—it's much more attractive to the eye if it follows out a theme. Supposing the buildings around it are stark, then you can go in one of two ways: either turn it into a riotous tangle of plants, a profusion of flowers and creepers—in short—a country garden in the middle of the city, or capitalise on the severity of its surroundings and give it a style, choosing only "architectural" plants with interesting shapes or with attractive leaves like the outspread hands of the Fatsia japonica, the sword-like spikes of the yucca.

Look to the Orient for ideas too; a Japanese theme is easy to achieve with a trellis of bamboo, perhaps echoed by bamboo furniture and—if you can find one—a pagoda-shaped ornament or small stone Buddha. Raid junk yards, and keep an eye open in the shops for something unusual that would make a focal point. Then build your patio around it: a lion mask on the wall, for instance, with water dribbling from it down into a basin, or a small pool—it doesn't have to be sunk into the ground—inset in a raised bed in the corner, surrounded by small plants like alpines—which are much better viewed off the ground at closer quarters.

Use colour with imagination too: walls don't have to be white or natural; they could be soft pink or creamy yellow. Flooring materials come in all sorts of colours besides plain grey and can be painted if you like; they should last at least a season. And when it comes to choosing plants, think in colour themes too; an all-white garden can look cool and sophisticated, or perhaps you might plan just one corner in blue. Aim to have at least one tree or shrub, if you can, that has colourful foliage in the autumn, and something that flowers in the winter, too. Remember to plant for scent, as well: perfumed climbers and perennials should be sited near to where you sit, or near the back door for the greatest pleasure.

Given your own plot to play with, you could turn it into the courtyard of a Turkish harem, a Mediterranean sun terrace, a medieval cloister or a Greek temple, provided you have the right set of props. Patterned ceramic tiles, large terra cotta pots, fake columns in reconstituted stone or even lightweight fibreglass; all these things are available. Let your imagination run riot. Don't thumb through the pages of gardening periodicals yet—that comes later. Concentrate instead on decoration magazines and pictures of stately homes and their gardens to see what is being done on a grander scale; it's amazing how magazines will spark off ideas.

How to Plan your Plot

Set it all down on paper first; you'll save unnecessary expense, and it's fun to do. Draw up an accurate plan on graph paper, marking in permanently sited things such as drainpipes, manhole covers, steps, doorways—anything that cannot be changed; unfortunately, it's easy to forget about them when you are away from the site. Mark the points of the compass on it, too, since it's foolish to plan for an exotic, rather tender shrub to go on a north-facing wall.

The next step is to mark any permanent planting places—raised beds, built-in troughs—before calculating how much paving concrete or tiling you need for the "floor." Finally come the cast of the show: the permanent trees and shrubs. Be sure to look up their eventual height before you rush out to buy. Growing them in tubs, it is true, may give a bonsai effect, but it is much better to pick something that is right for the scale of your plot. Try your trees and shrubs on the plan: look up their eventual spread in the catalogues, then pencil in the area they will take up; better still, cut out pieces of paper to scale. You may find you want to move them around, and it's much easier to do so on paper.

Try your plan in 3-D too. Take some photographs of your patio from every angle; then sketch in with a felt-tip pen all paving, plants, and structures, to discover how they will look.

A seating/dining area needs careful planning. (See page 18) You need an absolute minimum of 8 square feet for a table and four chairs; remember that those chairs will have to be pulled back so that the sitters can get at the table. Sometimes it is better to arrange for a built-in banquette to save a little space. Ideally the area needs to be sited near the kitchen door or, if you have one, a barbecue area.

Having once got your plan down on paper to your satisfaction, now try it out: using garden twine and sticks, peg out the actual sites of any flower beds, clusters of pot and troughs, retaining walls. This will show you just how much space you have left for the patio proper. If you are planning curved beds, then a garden hose can be snaked into their shape more easily, or you could dribble some sand on the ground to outline the area. But bear in mind that anything chalked out at ground level on the paving will appear to take up less room than the reality of the raised bed. Remember too, that you should calculate where raised beds are to be sited *before* you plan the flooring

(see pages 21–25) since beds are better sited on soil or hardcore than on solid stone.

When making your master plan, sketch in, as a reminder, a pipe for an outside tap or provision for outdoor lighting—any service item you might need. And remember that you may have to accommodate dustbins, a washing line, a way to the back gate, or storage for bicycles and toys. These mundane details do not mean, however, that you have to lose sight of your grand design; a shed can be turned into a Japanese pagoda or a temple with the aid of a little crafty carpentry for embellishments; and service items like dustbins and oil tanks can always be screened out of sight.

Aim for varied levels if you can, even on the smallest site. These not only give you bonus planting places in that extra dimension—up—but they also make the patio much more attractive to the eye, especially from indoors. Remember also to plan so that your patio looks good from the windows of your house or apartment; think of it in terms of a picture, framed by the window, when you make your plan since for some of the time you will be viewing it from indoors rather than out.

WHAT HAVE YOU GOT?

Planning a small space garden in a proper and professional way means that you have to take all kinds of factors into consideration. The *aspect,* for instance, is vitally important, for the way that a patio faces dictates everything about it. Obviously no one would want to plan a seating area against a wall facing north, for instance, where there is rarely if ever any sun. A south-facing patio is the best of all, if you are lucky to have one, for you will get sun almost all day. On the other hand this could be too much of a good thing in high summer, and you might need to plant some sort of overhead cover or shade, building a pergola to accommodate it. Or you might prefer to make some sort of awning which can be rolled up and down at will, according to the glare of the sun and its position overhead.

An east-facing patio will get sun in the morning—ideal for eating breakfasts out-of-doors, but probably shaded when evening comes; while one that faces west will get afternoon sun and is ideal for sitting out in the evening. If this is the case, plan to put in some scented flowers and climbers to make the most of it.

Another important consideration is *shade.* Many patios that ought to be sunny and well lit are in fact heavily shaded because they're in a city where other buildings blot out the light. The two types of shade dictate two different types of plants. The most common kind of shade on the patio is *damp shade:* the kind you find in basements and areas in front of houses that are below ground. Damp shade also encourages moss, algae and other growths that cause problems on stonework and need to be kept in check with the appropriate chemicals. If you are stuck with a damp area, then you're going to have to grow mainly foliage rather than flowering plants, relying on a few bright bedding plants in pots to liven things up from time to time. Ferns thrive in these conditions, as do hostas, ivy (Hedera) and hydrangeas. You can also grow camellias in these conditions and the ubiquitous Fatsia japonica. Many bulbs and woodland plants can take damp shade too. Lighten the patio as much as you possibly can by painting the walls—possibly the floor too—white. Consider installing a few mirrors on walls too, to reflect what light there is.

Dry shade is usually found where one or more overhanging trees shut out the light on your patio. Sometimes you can deal with this through a little neighbourly co-operation. More often than not, however, the shade remains. If the tree is deciduous, at least you should get reasonable light in the winter months when it is most needed. If the tree is in your plot, or very near it, its roots have penetrated underground, greedily draining all the nutrients out of your soil—bear that in mind when you come to plant. Never try to sow a lawn under conditions like these; although there are some grasses specially developed for sowing under trees, in a city they are unlikely to thrive. You should, however, be able to grow most annual flowers, shrubs like euonymus and holly (Ilex), and a large number of herbs, especially sage.

Exposure is another problem you may have to tackle—quite obvious if you have a windswept site. Less obvious, though equally destructive to gardens built in cities, are the down-draughts and funneling winds from nearby buildings. In addition, if your patio is sited on a flat roof, you'll find that all prevailing winds are fiercer at that height than at ground level. The best way to shield a garden from exposure of this kind is not, as you might think, to build a solid brick wall, for this could deflect the winds and cause down-draughts. Instead a pierced wall—decorative concrete blocks, trellis, or even netting—will break the force of the wind but avoid eddies that might damage the plants beneath.

Slope is another consideration. If your plot slopes towards the back door, torrential rain could cause trouble. Check the slope with a spirit level before you start paving. Any form of flagstones or concrete requires a slight slope so that rainwater will run away rather than linger: 2 inches/5cm in every 6 feet/2m is the usual amount to allow. This slope of course should run away from the house. If your plot has a pronounced slope, consider terracing it on two levels, it will look more attractive that way for sitting and dining.

Privacy is something that matters greatly to some people and not at all to others. Most small gardens are overlooked in some way, sometimes by the upper floors of neighbouring buildings, sometimes, by neighbouring plots—if the dividing walls are low. You need some privacy if you plan to use your plot as an outdoor room; otherwise you will have the uneasy feeling that you are sitting out on a stage. Screening will also give you some shelter from prevailing winds and can also keep the rain off if you have some solid structure overhead.

Sometimes all that is needed is the illusion of privacy, even though other people might see you if they took the trouble to do so. An openwork trellis used as a screen gives a comfortable cosiness to a seating area and makes a splendid backdrop for plants, especially climbers. If you have some sort of overhead screening, you may want to grow deciduous climbers on it if it is alongside the house, since evergreens may make the rooms inside too dark in the winter. The cheapest kind of permanent screening is wooden fencing, but since that may not go with the general look of the patio, you may have to budget more for bricks or concrete to get the right look. Screening may also be needed to hide service items, as already mentioned, or to obscure an undesirable view at the end of your garden. Tower blocks and factories seem formidable, but you can usually blot them out successfully with screening around your sitting area rather than at the end of the garden. The nearer the screen itself to your eye, the more it hides things that are some distance away. (See also page 24.)

Soil is less of a problem on the patio; but if you are planning some built-in beds, you ought to find out what kind of soil you are working with. One way is to enquire of neighbours what grows best and to go from there. However, soil analysis kits are cheap to buy and fun to use—rather like a toy chemistry set. Alternatively you can now buy a meter to measure the level of acidity in the soil. Either way, the reading is in terms of pH. The lower the pH reading, the more acid your soil; the higher, the more alkaline. A pH reading of 7 means that your soil is neutral—a situation sometimes found in cities. An acid soil means that you can grown anything in the rhododendron family with great success; camellia, heather (Erica), many conifers and most forms of magnolia enjoy an acid soil, as do hydrangea, the witch hazel (Hamemelis mollis) and skimmia.

Many more trees and shrubs prefer a chalky soil with lime in it; the Prunus and Acer families, and many decorative flowering shrubs such as the butterfly bush (Buddleia), Mexican orange blossom (Choisya ternata) flowering currant (Ribes) and clematis. The lime content of a soil that is normally neutral or acid can be increased by builders' rubble that contains mortar. Remember this point if you are planting near newly built walls.

One or two obliging trees and shrubs will put up with any conditions—acid or alkaline. The birch (Betula), the hawthorn (Crataegus) the cotoneaster and the yew (Taxus) are four examples: you can plant them almost anywhere.

Given containers and troughs to plant in, you can choose your own custom-made soil. It pays, in any case, to buy compost rather than dig it from the garden; thus you have a planting medium free from weeds and made specifically for container growing. Also, if you dig clay soil from the garden it will dry out and bake hard in containers if not watered regularly; and in heavy rain it will retain water and turn sour. If you must use garden soil, try to get a lighter loam, or something sandy. It is easier to add nutrients and bulk to it than to work with clay. Bear in mind, if you are buying soil, that you can now get special mixes for trees and shrubs, for acid lovers, for anything from cacti to bonsai and ferns.

If you are really in doubt as to what to plant, consult your nearest garden centre where the staff will know what conditions you are working with. A local park is another useful place to discover what grows well in your locality. Though you can afford to experiment with bedding plants and small perennials, when you are buying your basic background framework—trees and shrubs—you can't afford to make an expensive mistake.

Drainage is an important consideration if you are planning permanent raised beds; rainwater or that from a hose pipe must be able to drain away properly, or the soil will become waterlogged and sour, the roots of the plants eventually rotten. If you are making raised beds with brick retaining walls, install "weep holes" at intervals in between courses of bricks or between individual bricks to drain away water. Do this by inserting short pieces of metal tubing (plumbing off-cuts are ideal into the mortar at about 24-inch/60-cm intervals. Drainage holes of this type should be cleaned out from time to time; simply poke a piece of cane into them to make sure they are clear. Bear in mind when making raised beds that the larger they are, the more effective. Too small and they will dry out quickly, little better than large

containers. They should not be so deep, however, that you cannot reach the back of them when gardening.

Pots and containers (see pages 36–43) will need some form of drainage, too, and should be off the ground so that the water can run away from holes in their base. Standing containers on small pieces of brick not only tends to make them unstable but looks rather unattractive, too, so try to build something permanent for them to sit on—either a narrow wooden plinth or several small tiles to keep the general look of the patio or terrace tidier. Hanging baskets need to be sited where they can be watered effectively without damage to the paving underneath. It often pays to put them over a clutch of containers or an existing raised bed so that water that runs away through those.

WHAT DO YOU WANT?

The way you plan your patio garden and plant it depend very much on how you intend to use it. Is it simply a tiny "picture" outside your window? Is it a play area for your children? Is it a sun-bathing spot? Or is it an outdoor room in which you'll spend as much time as possible? Do ask yourself these questions before you go too far in your planning.

If the space is very small indeed, then your "garden" may be nothing much more than a narrow balcony or a tiny yard that does little more than lead the way to a back gate. In this case you are looking upon your miniscule plot as a picture framed by and to be viewed from windows and doors. Think of yourself as a painter, filling in a blank canvas when you work out your planting. Instead of making an ordinary plan, do a picture instead, drawing outlines of plants and containers on a shape that corresponds with the area you will be viewing.

It's important to think in terms of varied levels in a very small space of this kind. You don't want rows of pots and troughs all at floor level, but some raised as high as waist level or even higher on an ornamental plinth. And although you may not have room for trees and shrubs in anything other than dwarf versions, you can help fill your canvas by using mop-headed versions of items like the bay tree, geraniums and fuchsias, which can be trained to grow that way. Creepers and climbers, too, will play an important part in filling up your picture.

You need also to have a focal point, something that catches the eye: a small statue, a tiny fountain, or simply an attractive container, ground level, imaginatively planted. And just as an artist has to choose colours carefully, you need to think through the flowers you'll be using in your plot. A riot of different colours could become a little confusing in a very cramped space, so try varying it from one season to another, with pinks at one time, oranges and yellows at another. Sow packets of cheap annual seeds into containers and the expense is minimal.

If you want to be clever you can use colour to create perspective, to make a very small plot appear to be deeper than it really is. Cheat a little with trellis on the side which narrows from top to bottom as it goes away from the eye, and you can create amazing illusions in a small space. Dark green or blue plants tend to recede when you look at them, as do mauve and silver ones; so if you plant those in the background it will create distance. Warm colours like oranges, yellows and reds, on the other hand, seem to come towards you, and should be reserved for planting right in front of your eyes. The size of plants can deceive, too; put large-leaved ones at the front, rather than at the back of your mini-garden, grading down to the smallest leaved plants of all at the rear. You can cheat still further by planting in the distance a dwarf version of a well-known tree—a cypress (Cupressus) for instance, and the eye, not thinking it is the usual size, assumes it is further away than it is.

Another way to stretch a small patio is to echo something from the room that it adjoins. Pick up the red in a cushion, a piece of wallpaper or a curtain indoors and match it with, for example, a pot of geraniums outside. Thus both the room and the patio will be linked, making both seem larger. Another trick is to take a well-known plant that grows both indoors and out—Fatsia japonica or ivy, for instance—and have one in the room and one on the patio linking the two spaces. A very small patio is best with plain, muted flooring, for the plants are necessarily the stars of the show. You can, however, go for fantasy and fun, just for a change, with a roll-out mat of fake grass to sit on in the summer time. This special outdoor carpeting can usually be ordered at a good garden centre.

If small children are around, the patio may have to do double duty as a play area. Plants in this case need to be tough; it is better to major on flowering shrubs than on delicate bedding plants. One compromise is to have one or two lightweight plastic containers of bright flowers (use a soil-less compost to make them easier to lift) and then hastily move them indoors when playtime comes.

A patio for children should have as smooth a surface as possible—no rocky paving stones to cause tumbles, no roughened surfaces to graze knees. Plants with spikes and prickles are obviously unsuitable, too. A patio can be planned in two stages, however, so that it can turn itself into an idyllic outdoor room for grownups when the children are older. A fibreglass pond let into the surface of the paving can be used as a sandpit instead for the first few years, until it is safe to be filled and planted as a miniature water garden. A climbing frame, if you choose one that is made of an attractive material and site it properly, can become a freestanding tower over which to grow all sorts of climbers when the children have finished with it; old-fashioned climbing roses, for instance, intertwined with clematis. A swing sited as near to the corner as is practicable can be turned into a leafy bower or part of a pergola with very little trouble; again it's just a matter of planning.

It's a good idea, also to plan some storage on or around the patio so that outdoor toys don't have to be taken inside at the end of the day. An ideal solution for smaller items is to make a built-in seat with a hinged lid somewhere on the patio. Later on, when the toys are discarded, it will be useful for storing all those gardening implements, packets, cartons, and odd bits and pieces. Finally that essential item when children are around—a washing line—can be incorporated happily into the patio plan if you buy a whirligig one; later it could be covered and used as an umbrella to provide welcome shade.

A patio that is to be used mainly for relaxing in the sun needs space for you to lie full-length when you want to—even if you only use fold-away sun beds rather than full-sized loungers. In these circumstances, plants are better at a lower level in case they deprive you of the sun. A built-in occasional table, in the form of a block of stone, is a useful accessory; at other times set a plant in a pot on top of it.

Water is restful when you're relaxing out of doors, so do arrange, if you can, to use some on your patio garden. (See pages 30–35.) Wherever you site your pond, pick a pump that is not so powerful that it will shoot sprays of water all over you. You can use water in many different ways. You could fit a decorative mask on the wall and have water trickling into a basin beneath. (A pump concealed at the bottom will send it up to the mask again via a hidden pipe.) Or you could have a small rocky waterfall tumbling down into a tiny pool in a corner. Or at the very least, you could have a tray of pebbles with water trickling over them. Moving water is more effective than a simple pond, and wonderful as a cooler on hot, sunny days.

Shade may have to be taken into account when you want to lounge on your patio. A free-standing umbrella can be difficult to anchor, so consider some form of overhead awning. Alternatively, use a large-leaved plant like the giant rhubarb (Rheum palmatum) sited where it will cast a shadow over someone lounging near ground level. If the patio gets long hours of sunlight, avoid painting everything brilliant white, or you may find you have a glare; a soft pastel is more restful to the eyes.

The main reason why most people build patios is to have an outdoor room, somewhere to sit with a book or a drink and—above all—somewhere to eat during the blissful warm summer days. When planning an outdoor room of this kind, two factors come into consideration: the aspect of your plot (i.e. does the sun reach it in the morning or the evening?) and when you are likely to use it. A family that is out at work all day is most likely to want to use the patio in the evenings, even at weekend when there are chores to be done. Make sure, first of all, that you have allocated adequate space for a table and chairs (see page 8) and that their placement is right in relation to the sun. With the table near the kitchen door, food can be passed out and dishes removed with a minimum of effort. Alternatively, you may need some sort of surface nearby where dishes can be stowed temporarily. Dining out calls for a barbecue, if you have space for one. This again needs careful planning: work out which way prevailing winds blow; you don't want smoke pouring into the house. And bear in mind when planting trees and shrubs that they should be a reasonable distance from the fire to avoid scorching or—at least—have leathery leaves, as do laurel or holly.

The ideal furniture for an outdoor room (see pages 44–46) is the kind that can stay out all year round since finding storage space inside can be a problem, especially if you only have a flat with no garage or shed. Wooden furniture looks good but must be made from hardwood if it is to survive; also its rather solid thick-set appearance may not go with the general "decor". Metal furniture may be heavy to move around, may need constant painting, and may be uncomfortable to sit on. Plastic furniture can these days be found in attractive designs, imitating anything from wood to Victorian wrought iron. The best choice is furniture made from fibreglass, for you need something heavy enough to stand up to occasional high winds and strong enough to stand the usual wear and tear. The main disadvantage with plastic is the fact that it does attract dirt and dust; thus, if you choose white or pastel shades you'll find it will need a frequent wash. If the space is small, consider buying stacking or fold-up tables and chairs; there are several attractive versions on sale both in plastic and metal. Alternatively look out for "film director" chairs which not only stow away but look good indoors too—or those made from extravagantly curled cane. Both come in handy if you have extra guests for dinner.

GROUNDWORK

The flooring is the first thing to be established when you start work on your small space garden, for it will tend to dominate the scene if the patio is at all large. Since grass is impracticable in a small space, especially if you are planning an outdoor room, you will probably decide on some form of solid foundation. The particular material you pick will depend on how much cash you have to spend.

By far the cheapest material is concrete, and if you can't run to ready-made slabs, if your patio is a strange or awkward shape, or if you are hoping to build in special features like a pond—concrete is probably your best choice. What you need for the job is a mix of 1 part cement, 2½ parts sand and 4 parts coarse aggregate—all these measurements are by volume—plus an old door or a large piece of board on which to make the mix. Stir the dry ingredients together thoroughly then add water little by little either from a hose or watering can, depending on the amount you are mixing. Keep turning the whole heap over again and again with a spade until all the dry ingredients are absorbed. Don't let it get too wet or it will take a long time to dry. Lay your concrete on a solid base of about 6 inches/15 cm of compacted hardcore rubble. It doesn't have to be totally smooth and plain grey; you can divide it up into mock flagstones, marking out the squares with a board when the concrete is firm but not set, and you can push cobbles or other decorative pieces of stone into it at the same stage. You can also colour your cement

in several different pastel shades, if you want to.

Slightly more costly than concrete are pre-cast flagstones—not just in squares and circles but in rectangular and hexagonal shapes too. They come in differing thicknesses, sizes and colours. And if you can afford them, slabs are available made from reconstituted stone slabs; these weather very well, looking after just a few months as though they have been in place for generations. You need the same base of hardcore or rubble to start with; then the stones are set either in a layer of several inches of builders' sand or in a weak dry cement mix: 1 part cement to 9 parts sand is fine. It's vital to check that each slab is level as you lay it; use a spirit level, laying it both across and down to make sure all is well. A mix of sand or weak dry cement should then be brushed in between the slabs to help hold them in place.

Bricks, particularly second hand ones that have weathered a little, make a good flooring for a small space garden adjoining a country cottage or old house. They are, however, more tricky to lay; it pays to bring in a professional for the job, especially if you have a large number to lay. There are a number of patterns to choose from: the simple stretcher bond that is normally used for walls; a herringbone pattern or a basket weave, which are more complicated. They need to be bedded, ideally in a mix of sand and cement. The disadvantages are that bricks do become slippery when wet and tend to attract moss, especially if the patio is shaded.

Gravel—though not used very much for patios in this country—can be very effective. It has the advantages of being easy to lay and cheap to buy; it also comes in several shades: white, brown, black, or yellow—or a mix or all four. Choose the largest-sized gravel you can find because it is much easier to keep tidy and less likely to be trodden indoors. You need to lay gravel to a depth of slightly less than 1 inch/2.5 cm on compacted soil or hardcore, then go over it with a garden roller if you have one. Gravel is best if it is contained in some way, either by wood framing or by bricks laid on their sides.

Wooden decking in another unusual choice for a patio and has much to commend it if you are working with an uneven or sloping site. Wooden decks are laid like floors, on joists which run in the opposite direction to the planking; these joists must be fixed on supports of strong timber. Planking for a patio deck should be spaced at least ¼ inch/5 mm apart to allow the rain to run away and not form puddles on the wood. All timber used for decking must be well-seasoned and treated against rot. If you are laying decking directly on the ground, put a layer of thick polythene sheeting between the wooden planks and the ground. All sorts of patterns can be used for a wooden deck: parquet, for instance, or—simpler to lay and lovely to look at—diagonal lines. Edge your decking with a railing in the same type of wood to give it an attractive finish.

If your patio is big enough, think of combining two or more materials to make the flooring look more interesting: large squares of concrete framed by rows of bricks, for instance, or even ceramic tiles set into solid concrete to mark out certain special areas. Another good idea is to use several different sizes or shapes of one material: rectangular paving slabs mixed with square ones, for example. If you are using paving stones, consider leaving one out here and there, and substituting a square of pebbles or gravel, or setting in a large container. You could even make a built-in pond this way. Leaving out the occasional flagstone means that you could also grow attractive alpines underfoot, or little squares of green; use chamomile rather than grass since it doesn't need cutting. Consider finishing off the edges of a solid patio with a low retaining wall made from two parallel courses of brick or stone, and fill the gap between them with soil. You can then grow alpines and crevice plants on them.

Flooring for balconies and patios at roof height needs careful consideration. Before embarking on an ambitious scheme it is as well to check that the area you are planning to garden can take the extra weight involved. Many flat roofs were scarcely made for walking on, let alone for heavy containers filled with soil; check with a surveyor, or you could find yourself in trouble with the neighbours. The area which will take most of the strain is the centre of the patio so it is not a good principal to put trees in tubs or anything heavy in that position.

Even a reinforced roof should not have more than about 12 inches/30 cm of soil on it. To be safe, however, reduce the weight by using soil-less or peat-based compost, which is much lighter to handle and, instead of edging beds with bricks or stone, choose peat blocks instead. Flooring for a roof patio may cause problems as you can't lay down anything permanent in case of leaks, which would be difficult to detect. Many roofs are covered with a bituminous preparation which is sticky and unpleasant to walk on in hot weather. For this reason wooden decking makes the best choice for a roof garden, since it can be made up in sections and taken up as necessary for inspection of the roof surface underneath.

While you are constructing the floor of your patio, don't forget to position any posts you may want for a pergola, for overhead shelter, or to host a special climbing plant. It is much easier to set them into the ground at this stage than to hack up paving stones later on. The slimmest, least obtrusive supports for any form of overhead shelter are made of metal, but they don't look attractive and should only be used if

placed out of view or if covered by a growing plant. Wooden posts are the most usual choice and should be well treated with preservative *before* they are put in place, rather than afterwards when vital areas around joints or below ground might be missed. Don't skimp on wooden supports; use the best timber you can afford and; if it is to support any weight overhead it should measure at least 4 × 4 inches/10 × 10 cm. Posts should be set in concrete in the ground—up to 3ft deep if they are taking any weight.

Free-standing screening, as opposed to a traditional fence, should also be set solidly in the ground in a similar way. Remember that it will have to take considerable stress in high winds, added to which will be the weight of climbers and wall shrubs pinned against it.

Whatever the type of flooring and framework you use for your patio, try to choose something that fits in with its general theme, with its surroundings, and with the house. Plain concrete looks badly out of place alongside a period home, while brickwork might be too fussy with a modern apartment. And when it comes to picking containers and troughs (see pages 36–43), make sure that they are compatible with the flooring on which they are going to stand. Terra cotta, for instance, tends to clash with red brick but looks better against tinted concrete; containers that are made from natural wood go well with decking and with brick but not with cement paving. When you are laying your floor, then, consider making up some containers in similar material for a built-in look. It is easy to construct a small square container for plants out of bricks, or you could be more adventurous and try a circular one. Old stone sinks go well with genuine flagstones, and it is easy to make a small container with drystone walls around it. Concrete is even more versatile; you can actually cast concrete troughs by using two wooden boxes, one larger than the other. Set the smaller box squarely inside the larger one, making sure that the gap all round is several inches wide. Pour 2–3 inches/5–7.5 cm concrete in the base of the larger box; set the smaller one carefully and centrally on top of this just before it has set, then pour in more of the concrete mix round the sides. When the concrete has set, just strip off the wood and the trough is ready to use. If you want to incorporate drainage holes, set some pieces of metal tubing into the base concrete, making sure that they are kept clear.

Large, wooden Versailles tubs, which are basically square, are also easy to make and are good containers for small trees. If you are constructing your own, it's a good idea to make it so that one side panel slides out—useful when you want to inspect the roots of the tree, move it out of the container, or replace some of the soil.

WHAT ABOUT THE WALLS?

Climbing plants make the most out of a very small plot; for the ground space they occupy they give a magnificent show, clothing the walls fast and, on occasions, hiding an ugly view. They can also be used successfully to soften up the stark lines of an unattractive fence, or to link it with a building. And if you eat out-of-doors, a climber will quickly cover a pergola overhead, giving it an exotic touch.

With a little cunning, it's possible to have a good display from climbers all year round if you select some for their flowers, some for their foliage, and some for winter berries. You can also pick some for their perfume: winter jasmine (Jasminum nudiflorum) and honeysuckle varieties (Lonicera) for the high summer. They can be grown in tubs or troughs if there is not an actual flower bed for them (though they won't make so much growth that way). You can also use them for ground cover plants— something few people think of—letting them spill over a flower bed, smothering weeds instead of climbing up a wall. Another decorative effect is to let one climber act as host to another—a rose, for instance, supporting a clematis.

The most important factor, however, when choosing your climbers is to make sure that they are right for your site. Aspect is crucial; so find out first whether the walls you're planning to plant against are cool and shady or hot and dry.

A cool wall (north- and east-facing in Britain) almost certainly lacks sunshine and may be exposed to biting winds as well. Plants there have to be chosen with care; fortunately, though, quite a large range of climbers and wall shrubs thrive in these conditions because they like the perpetually damp soil and cool root-runs that they get. You can't grow some of the showier flowers against a cool wall, but you can go for berries and fruit; the morello cherry, for instance, is very happy here. However, surprisingly, the larger-flowered clematis and several of the old-fashioned climbing roses can cope. (See pages 50–52).

A warm, sunny wall (south-facing in Britain) is the only place to try plants which are not totally hardy in this country; hence it is very good for wall fruits like figs, nectarines, peaches and grapes. But remember to water properly since sunny walls tend to dry out amazingly quickly after the rain. A sheltered, sunny wall (west-facing in Britain) is best for plants that are likely to be attacked by frost such as the camellia. Many plants with delicate flowers suffer from frost burn when early morning sun shines on frozen petals, but a wall that receives most of the sun at the end of the day makes an ideal spot in which to grow them. This is also the right place in which to plant wisteria, which must never be allowed to dry out.

Most climbers that you are likely to grow around the patio cling to a support either by twining round it, attaching themselves with tendrils or, in a very few cases such as ivy and virginia creeper (Parthenocissus quinquefolia) by sticking to a wall by their aerial roots. Supports vary: a series of nails in the wall, possibly with wires threaded from one to another; a trellis; or solid, plastic-coated mesh. Some lightweight, flimsy climbers—such as morning glory (Ipomoea)—which are also annuals can be grown against lightweight plastic netting without heavier support. Remember when you put up your trellis or fix your mesh in place that, once established, climbers can become quite weighty; thus make sure that the support fence or wall is stoutly built and the support for the climbers fixed to it securely. (See page 24). Never nail a trellis straight against a wall or fence; it should stand slightly away from it (the usual trick is to fix wooden blocks on the wall first, then nail the trellis to them). You do this for two reasons: to allow air to circulate around the back of the growing plant thereby avoiding fungal diseases like mildew, and to protect the trellis itself, which is then less likely to stay damp and rot. For the same reason any wooden structure that is fixed to a wall should stop just short of the ground, or it will tend to rot around the base.

If you are planning to grow climbers up a wall that needs to be painted regularly, there are two ways of handling the situation: you can train the plants up ropes which can then be detached at the top and swung out of the way when painting time comes round, or you can hinge the trellis at the bottom so that both trellis and accompanying plant can be laid flat on the ground.

Remember that your climbers will be in place for a long time, forming the part of the permanent framework of your patio, so you want to give them the best possible start in life. This means a soil rich in humus to feed the roots. If the bed into which they are to be put consists of nothing much more than tired old city soil, dig in plenty of compost, fertiliser—whatever you can get—to make it fertile and receptive. If you are planting in a container, then pick the appropriate compost for that plant.

Next check the site carefully; dig down to make sure that there are neither drains near the surface that might interfere with the root-run, nor builders' rubble—often the case if the wall is newly built. Don't plant your climber right on the corner of a building where it might be exposed to draughts; put it at least two feet in. And when you dig a hole for it, don't make the common mistake of setting it right up close to the wall. This is for two reasons: it may not get its fair share of moisture since—with a tall wall in

particular—rain may be deflected away from the base; also, hot sunlight may scorch not just the stems and leaves by bouncing back from the wall, but the roots as well. And, jammed up against a wall, the roots only have a semi-circle instead of a full circle in which to grow. Hence site your climber about 6 inches/15 cm away if it has to be tied in to a trellis, and 1–2 feet/30–60 cm if it is technically a wall shrub and supports itself.

Container-grown climbers and wall shrubs can be planted at almost any time of the year; in winter months however, you should use your common sense and not attempt to put them in on a frosty day. Leave the plants, in their pots, somewhere cool but frost-free until you are ready to install them. They won't come to any harm provided you keep the soil in the pot just damp, not water-logged. When planting day arrives, dig a generous hole *before* you attempt to move the plant from its container; never leave it lying around with roots exposed. Dig a hole at least 2 feet square and 2 feet/60 cm deep and—if the soil looks sticky—throw in a little shingle, some broken crocks or some peat to help with drainage. A container-grown plant should be put into the ground just as it is, unless an excessive number of roots is wrapped round the outside of the soil ball. If this is the case, try teasing a few of them out, carefully. If they are fixed fast, however, leave them as they are. Set the plant carefully into the bottom of the hole, making sure that it is firm on the base of the soil, and scatter a little bone meal around it to encourage the roots to venture out in search of food.

If the plant has to be temporarily staked until it is tall enough to be tied to a support, the stake should go

in before the plant does, to make sure that you do not accidentally spear the roots. With a container-grown plant you then simply fill carefully the gaps in the hole, making sure that the soil level of the root ball tallies with that of the ground around it, then press it in place with the sole of your shoe.

Some plants arrive bare-rooted, i.e. simply wrapped in a little moss or packing and polythene.

Roses are often sold this way, as are those from specialist growers. Having sized up the plant and the general shape that the roots make, and having dug a hole to accommodate them, unwrap the climber and set it in the hole, fanning its roots out like the spokes of an umbrella. In this case make sure that you set the base of the stem on a little mound of soil in the bottom of the hole and to avoid an air pocket underneath. Throw several spadefuls of soil over the roots; then give the plant a little shake to make sure the earth drops between the individual roots; then cover it with soil, making sure that you do not go above the natural mark on the stem that shows the depth at which the plant was grown.

All climbers and shrubs should be given a good soak before they are planted, then watered again once in the ground. Keep an eye on them for a week or two to make sure that they don't dry out.

Some climbers simply romp away once you put them into the ground; others are much slower growers. The climbing hydrangea (Hydrangea petiolaris) often makes little or no growth at all in its first season but is worth persevering with since it will grow on a cold, shaded wall. The wisteria, too, may be disappointing at first, but both these plants make up for lost time once they are established.

Sometimes a really fast-growing climber is needed to cover an eyesore in a hurry, to provide instant greenery of for overhead shade. The fastest is the russian vine (Polygonum baldschuanicum) which will easily make 20 feet/6 m of growth in one season. It needs careful siting for it invades gutters, openings, and drains; still, kept under control it is an invaluable friend and can either be pruned back hard in the winter to encouraged fewer thicker, gnarled, vine-like stems, or clipped like a hedge. If you are at all uncertain of your ability to cope but do need some quick greenery, try growing one in a container, which will curb its excess energy.

Another very fast grower that you might like to try is the hop (Humulus lupulus) which attaches itself to anything—other plants if necessary—by its slightly adhesive, prickly stem and leaves. The Japanese hop (Humulus japonicus) is the fastest variety to choose but will not always stand the winter in cold or exposed sites and is therefore often grown as an annual.

Finally, for a riot of colour on the walls, especially during your first summer when your permanent climbers are still finding their way, invest in some packets of seed. Grow morning glories (Ipomoea) sweet peas (Lathyrus odoratus) and nasturtiums (Tropaeoleum) in profusion: cheap and cheerful plants that never let you down.

WATER ON THE PATIO

One of the most exciting features you can add to your patio is water used in some way or other. Whether in a pool, a fountain, or a basin it gives constant movement and interest and mirrors the sky, too, adding more light to the scene.

Patio ponds can be bought pre-formed, or dug out and lined either with concrete for a permanent job or with heavy-duty butyl, which will last a number of years. The home-made variety gives you endless scope for incorporating water into the main design. Generally a traditional yard or patio in a rectangle looks best with a pond that is also rectangular or square. If you are using paving, it's a relatively easy matter to miss out one or two squares and put a pond in their place. Make your pond before you do the paving and you will be able to take the water just a little—an inch is probably enough—under the edge of adjoining flagstones so that the edge of the plastic lining is well hidden.

Dig a hole for the patio pond, making the sides slope outwards a little, or go up in steps to avoid a tendency to cave-in. Calculate how much butyl lining you'll need by this simple rule: measure the length and width of the hole, then add *twice* the depth of the hole to each measurement. In other words, if your pool is to be 2 feet/60 cm wide, 3 feet/90 cm long and 1½ feet/45 cm deep, you add 1½ feet/45 cm twice to the 2 feet/60 cm width, 1½ feet/45 cm twice again to the 3 feet/90 cm length, making 5 feet × 6 feet/1.5 m × 1.8 m, totalling 30 square feet/2.7 square metres in all.

Choose a warm day to line your pond; leave the butyl out in the sun and it will be more flexible to handle. Line the hole first with an old piece of carpeting or underfelt if you have some, as this will prevent the odd sharp stone from puncturing the plastic, then set the butyl carefully and centrally over the pond site. Anchor the cut the edge round the side with bricks or heavy stones at this stage before you start to put in the water; otherwise you may find the plastic gets dragged underwater so that you have to start again. As the pond fills the butyl will take the shape that you have carved out for it, and you can adjust the weights round the edge. Once the pond is full, trim away any surplus plastic, leaving about 8 inches/20 cm, which should be buried in the surrounding soil. Finally put the flagstones in place, making sure that they overlap slightly. If your pond is large enough you can make a shallow shelf by cutting a step out of the side, just below water level, for marginal plants.

What sized pool should you have? You can't really keep both plants and fish in anything less than 30 square feet/2.7 square metres in area, and your pond should be at least 1½ feet/45 cm deep if you are keeping fish in it; otherwise it may freeze over in the winter time. Don't put your patio pond in the shade if you want to grow water lilies, for they must have adequate light to flower; and don't put it under a deciduous shrub or tree unless you are prepared to clean it regularly to get rid of dead and decaying leaves. Use black or beige butyl for the lining, it looks more natural than swimming pool blue and black makes the pond look deeper than it really is. And don't carve out lots of curves unless you are prepared to spend some time folding and tucking the plastic to accommodate them.

Pre-formed fibreglass pools are in some ways more difficult to install than butyl ones, for sand or soil must be packed carefully around them to stop them from rocking as you fill them. Use a spirit level all the time when putting in a pre-formed pool; nothing looks worse than a tipsy pool with one side higher than the other, exposing all the plastic.

As an alternative to the conventional built-in pool, think in terms of turning unusual containers into free-standing ponds an old kitchen copper, a tin bath, an old sink. An urn with its drainage holes plugged makes a magnificent free-standing pond and is just large enough to take one miniature water lily. Or you can now buy ready-made containerised ponds that look as though they have walls built from brick. They come in rounds, half-rounds and rectangles and are made from specially cast resin which reproduces the original colour and texture of brick and stone.

Water gardens are also becoming popular on the patio—shallow pools built as part of the patio itself, just a few inches deep with water running over decorative pebbles. A water garden can also take the form of a canal running along the side of the patio, with a bridge—if necessary—leading out into the rest of the garden. Water features of this kind can be turned into mini-streams or canals if you install a pump in one end with a hidden pipe at the other to

return the water to the pump again.

To keep your pool in peak condition you'll need a hard-working team of aquatics—water plants to clean and oxygenate it. Left to itself, a pond soon becomes like a bowl of pea soup, as sunlight on the water soon causes algae to form. The way to tackle this problem is to make sure you have oxygenators in your pool; they will deprive the algae of any nutrients in the water and, in causing underwater shade, any light. As their name suggests, oxygenators also return oxygen to the water and use up carbon dioxide given off by fish and decaying vegetable matter. You need at least one oxygenator to every square foot of water surface. Many pond plant specialists supply suitable plants for ponds of different sizes they come in kits ready to create the right balance.

Deep water plants like the water lily can be put directly into soil at the bottom of a pool, but since this tends to make the water murky a container is normally used. You can buy special plastic baskets for water plants though an ordinary plastic flower pot will do equally well and generally contains the soil more securely. If you do use a basket, line it first with a piece of sacking to help keep in the soil.

Be careful what soil you choose for your water plants. You want to give them a good start in life but special potting compost is not a good choice in this case because it may contain chemical fertiliser or some form of mineral that could be poisonous in water, especially to goldfish. A light, sandy or peat-based soil is unsuitable too, for it may float away and make the pond unattractive. A heavy clay-like loam is best of all, and you can buy packets of special pond soil from some garden centres.

Once your aquatics are planted they will need extra help to stay in place underwater, so scatter some gravel on the surface of the soil. If you are also stocking fish, make sure that the gravel is of a large grade, or the fish may move it and possibly swim off with it.

Don't worry if your water lily disappears to the bottom of the pond when you plant it; it will grow a longer stem in an amazingly short time to bring its leaves up to the surface of the water. Many people mistakenly believe that you have to set its container on something and gradually lower the plant to the bottom—over a period of several weeks—but this is a fallacy.

If you want your patio pond to look well established in a very short time, do plan for some marginal plants: those that grow in just a few inches of water. One valuable task they perform is to hide hard edges as well as the evidence of plastic sheeting where it is most likely to show—just above the surface of the water. If you haven't made a shelf for them to grow on, you can use any suitably shaped con-tainer—a rectangular plastic window box, for instance, placed on a pile of bricks or some other sort of column to lift it to the surface of the water. Rushes and reeds look best, with flowers in season. You could grow cottongrass (Emophorum) which looks good in a small space, or the marsh marigold (Caltha palustris) too. Marginal plants are also useful to hide pond lighting, for you can put specially made lamps among them to highlight the pool (See pages 6 and 46.)

Fountains are fine provided you get the right size for your pond; one with too fierce a pump will shower everyone with spray no matter how hard you try to turn it down. Bear in mind, however that water lilies prefer to grow in still water, so if you're combining the two, put the fountain up one end of the pond rather than in the middle. If it sprays a nearby flower-bed constantly, consider putting bog plants in it for an attractive display; dig up the soil, put down a layer of plastic to help conserve moisture, then replace it. Some kinds of fern, notably the royal fern (Osmunda regalis) love damp soil and would thrive there, as would some of the woodland plants—primulas for instance, provided they have some shade. The umbrella plant (Peltiphyllum peltatum) would also grow in these conditions.

Having well established your patio pond, do remember that it will need maintenance as does any other form of garden. It will quickly look drab and neglected especially if you allow autumn leaves, grass cuttings and other vegetable matter to float on the surface and eventually sink, only to decay at the bottom of the pond. Remember, too, to remove the heads of water lilies and other pond plants as soon as the flowers have died, or they too will decay in the water. If you are going away for a while, or if you are not using the patio, consider investing in a fine-mesh net which could be pegged in place over the surface of the pond, allowing fish and vegetation to breathe and grow but keeping out falling foliage.

Clean your pond by raking it across the surface—use a wooden rake if you can find one—and give flowering plants a feed every summer once they are established. They thrive on bone meal: mix it in with a little heavy soil and water and press pellets of it into the soil in the plant's container.

From time to time you will find that your pond is beginning to look rather overgrown. Tackle this problem just as you would with perennials in the garden: rake up submerged aquatics and divide them, and do the same for marginal plants.

Whether to heat your patio pool or not in the winter depends on whether or not you keep fish. Remember: the more shallow the pool, the more likely it is to freeze. Fortunately, small pond heaters can be bought that run on very little electricity and keep the water at the right temperature.

CONTAINERS

Growing plants in containers—on the patio on their own or to top up permanent beds—has a number of advantages. You can switch them around as you wish, changing colour schemes from one month to another, and you can plant on several different levels if you choose a mix of low-standing troughs and higher tubs. Plants in containers can be crammed in to give the luxuriant look that is often difficult to achieve in a single flower bed. And when things are past their best—bulbs, for instance, that have flowered—it's easy to move them away out of sight.

It's important to choose the right kind of container to suit your particular patio, ornate old-fashioned ones such as decorative urns may be attractive in their own right but totally out of place in a modern setting.

Plain containers made from concrete or plastic, on the other hand, need to be well planted if they are not to look uninspiring and dull.

It always pays to get the largest possible containers that the space will take, for they won't dry out so quickly in the summer or require frequent watering. If however your patio is on a balcony or a roof garden you have to consider whether something heavy may be out of the question. Really large containers are best set on a mini-trolley made from a square of wood with casters, if they are ceramic, or with casters fixed to their base if they are made from wood. Alternatively if you are only likely to move them occasionally, you can tilt the container to one side, slip a stout piece of sacking underneath, and drag them along on that. Always try your container in place empty,

when it's much lighter to move around, to make sure that you've picked the right spot.

Plastic has now superceded earthenware as the most popular material for plant pots and tubs. It has many advantages; it is cheap, light, and holds water longer in the soil. It can be moulded into all kinds of interesting shapes including "tower" pots which slot into one another, skyscraper fashion, with plants growing out of their sides. The main disadvantage of plastic is that it does not look particularly pretty and is best used with trailing plants down its sides also it becomes brittle after a long time in the sun and will eventually start to crack.

Terra cotta or clay pots look attractive but need careful handling because they break easily; moisture evaporates through them, too, so they need watering more frequently. Ordinary flowerpots are relatively cheap, but anything more sophisticated is expensive. Wooden pots look attractive in country surroundings but need constant maintenance to prevent rot. They have the advantage, however, of keeping the roots of plants warmer in winter than other types of container. If you are handy with a saw you can make simple wooden troughs for yourself; you should choose a hardwood if they are to last at all.

Fibre glass pots are usually moulded to look like lead, stone or some other material. They are extremely expensive initially but will last well and can be very attractive indeed. You will also find troughs and urns made from reconstituted stone (crushed stone mixed with cement). These look good but are extremely heavy. They should last a long time, though they occasionally crack in hard frosts.

A new lightweight container can now be bought cheaply to last one season. Made from resin-bonded cellulose, it looks as if it is moulded out of compressed peat. This container can be used as a liner for a large pot or hanging basket, or set as it is on the patio—useful when you want something to fill in odd corners and are not overly concerned about appearances. Be warned, however, the largest sizes are fragile when filled with soil; lift one to try and move it, and it may split.

Of course you don't have to buy containers made specifically for your plants. Be inventive; follow the southern Mediterranean fashion and save large tins and oil cans to use as planters; paint them bright colours with odds and ends left over from home decorating. Old wooden wheelbarrows have become so popular as plant holders that one manufacturer is now making small ones specially for that purpose. Old sinks are excellent for alpines and other small plants. One of the cheapest large containers you can use is a full-sized plastic bucket, preferably in

black. Leave the handle unobtrusively at the back; it will come in handy when you want to move the container. For ideas on how to make your own containers, see page 24.

Hanging baskets and half baskets look attractive and give you the chance to display colour at a higher level. But they need frequent watering—as often as twice a day in mid-summer—so don't hang them over a sitting area or where people are likely to pass.

The easiest way to water hanging baskets is to lash a piece of cane to the end of a length of hose to support it, hold the other end of the cane, and you can direct the flow of water into the basket. Another alternative is to hang the basket on a block and tackle (obtainable from yachting shops) so that you can lower it for watering. Wire baskets which are lined with plastic or resin-bonded cellulose rather than moss, and solid baskets moulded from plastic with just a few holes in their sides need less watering than the others.

Having chosen your container, don't be tempted to try and save cash by filling it with ordinary garden soil. Specially made compost—quite apart from having been formulated for plants in pots—is sterile, so you won't be bothered with weeds. This is particularly important if you are sowing annuals, when it would be difficult to know at first which is weed, and which is flower. Plants in containers are like caged birds, relying on us totally for food and most of their water. So while the roots of plants put straight into the ground can search for the nutrients they want, those in a pot are confined; and a pot of garden soil is unlikely to give them everything they need. Soil-less composts on sale now have the great advantage of being lightweight. They're not suitable, however, for a large plant in a lightweight container such as one of plastic, for as the compost dries out, the plant will probably topple over. Remember you can buy special compost for acid-loving plants, for trees and shrubs—even for cacti, so you are not limited to the type of soil in your garden.

When filling your containers with compost, it is best to put a layer of gravel or broken crocks in the bottom to help drainage. If for some reason the container has no drainage holes in it, add a few pieces to charcoal to help keep the soil sweet.

Although not technically containers, growing bags are a great boon if you want to grow something temporarily on the patio—salad crops, for instance, or a special display of plants like dahlias or sweet peas. Growing bags can be disguised if you put a row of bricks round their sides, with large pebbles over the top. Don't throw them away at the end of the season; the compost can be used for containers provided you top up the fertiliser in it. Growing bags are particularly useful if you are away a great deal, for you can buy them in a self-watering version with a reservoir built in. There are also drip-feed systems specially formulated for watering growing-bags in your absence. And even the basic model holds water better than the average container since part of its top is covered by plastic.

What should you plant in your containers? The large sizes can take trees, shrubs, and climbers. Although they won't grow as large as they would in the open ground (since their roots are confined) you can raise some splendid specimens; many kinds of conifers; evergreens such as camellia, rhododendron, or viburnum and others which have foliage that turns colour in the autumn—some of the maples, for instance, and amelanchiers. Use your common sense when buying trees for containers, don't pick those which are expected to reach 40 feet/12 metres after a number of years; instead stick to those that are small. Climbers including wisteria do well in tubs; wisteria can be trained successfully into a weeping standard shape with a little patience.

Topiary in tubs is fun with either the traditional yew (Taxus), box (Buxus) or the evergreen honey-suckle (Lonicera nitida). Train them by twisting wire around their stems then bending them; you will be able to clip them into simple shapes in a very short time. Don't forget the shrub-like herbs that make splendid large container plants; lavender (Lavandula) and rosemary (Rosmarinus). Both of these can be clipped into interesting shapes, too.

Flowers all year round are perfectly possible with the help of containers. Start the year with a crop of bulbs, which will take you through until the following spring, by May the first of the bedding plants—alyssum and aubretia—should be blooming, and cottage garden flowers like columbine (Aquilegia) the wallflower (Cheiranthus) and forget-me-not (Myosotis palustris) which you need to sow in the autumn of the previous year. Throughout the summer plenty of bedding plants are available, raised indoors from seed if you have the space—geraniums, fuchsia, petunias and so on. If any of your containers are in the shade, then go for busy Lizzie (Impatiens) and begonias, which will thrive in those conditions. Many kinds of lillies bloom throughout the summer (in the case of nerines until November) and make splendid specimen plants and tubs. A mixture of standard and trailing geraniums look good year-round, too, and you can use the same technique with fuchsia—simply select a straight-stemmed plant and take off all side shoots until it reaches the height you want (you need to tie it to a bamboo stake); then let it bush out at the top like a standard rose.

Winter flowers are more difficult to come by. Bridging the gap between the last of the chrysanthe-mums and the arrival of snowdrops and crocuses is best done with winter flowering shrubs instead; winter jasmine (Jasminum nudiflorum) witch hazel (Hamamelis mollis) and Daphne mezereum, all of

which can be grown in large tubs, then used to support annual climbers or bedding plants during the summer months.

When plants are crammed together, as they are in containers, watch carefully for pests, which may spread like wildfire in these conditions. It pays to spray your plants regularly against aphids, in particular; and on hot dry summer days, keep an eye open for the red spider mite—mist your plants regularly to discourage it from taking a hold.

THE FINISHING TOUCH

It's amazing how easy it is to make an attractive living area on even the smallest patio, if you experiment a little. If you've space for a chair or two, better still a table as well, you can make eating out-of-doors an extra dimension in your life.

Patio furniture needs to be chosen with care. It should be light and small enough to stow away when not in use or durable enough to be left out at all times of year. A third possibility is the kind of furniture that you can bring indoors and use in the house.

Wooden furniture, provided it is made from hardwood specially treated against rot, can be left out all year round. Unfortunately properly made garden furniture in wood may be large and heavy and is not always suitable for a small patio. What you can sometimes find, however, are very cheap second-hand wooden chairs intended for the house that can be either painted or treated with preservative for use on the patio. They won't last indefinitely, of course, but if they cost next to nothing in the first place they can almost be regarded as disposable. The furniture wouldn't have to consist of matching items either, for you could paint it all the same colour.

Metal furniture will stand up well to the elements provided it is made either of a non-rusting material like cast aluminium or painted or coated with plastic. It has the disadvantages of being heavy to move around and uncomfortable to sit on, though this can soon be remedied with the aid of cushions. Some attractive "antique" furniture can be found in cast iron or cast aluminium made from original moulds during the eighteenth to nineteenth century. It is

expensive but will of course last indefinitely and goes well with a patio that adjoins an old house. If on the other hand you have a modern patio garden, look out for attractive folding dining chairs in metal with wooden slatted seats, matched by a table made in a similar way. They come in white and all sorts of cheerful colours and look bright on grey and sunny days.

Plastic furniture is by far the cheapest to buy and is now made in convincing imitations of wood and cast iron; many of the chairs are stackable. If your patio is in an exposed spot, make sure that the plastic furniture you buy is heavy enough to stand up to high winds, or it may take off in a gale.

Cane furniture looks luxurious and takes up rather a lot of room, but it is light and easy to move around. However, it will not last more than a season or so if you leave it out in the rain, and is really only suitable if you can find houseroom for it when the weather is inclement. Even if it has been treated against showers, it will swiftly lose its sheen and turn an unattractive grey.

Use your imagination when furnishing the patio; make your own tables, for instance, by searching junk shops for an unusual base, then fitting a top on it. The iron work tables into which treadle sewing machines were fitted can often be found for next to nothing, and with a slab of marble on top make excellent patio furniture. A large, turned column of wood that once formed part of a newel post for a flight of stairs could form the base of a pedestal table, as could a tall wooden stool.

You can also make your own wooden furniture, incorporating storage space; create simple wooden cubes with hinged, cushioned lids to make attractive outdoor stools that go round a table and stow away underneath it when not in use. Inside them, provided no children use the patios, you can store boxes and tins of garden chemicals and fertilisers, small tools, and packets of seed. Otherwise, use them for toys. If there is space to spare you could build in a bench with a similarly hinged seat against a wall to take larger items like forks and spades, rakes.

If you have only a really small space for eating out on the patio, consider making a table that is hinged on the wall and flaps down when out of use. This, plus some stools or stackable/folding chairs, will take up little room and still allow you to eat out-of-doors.

Some kind of permanent lighting is a worthwhile investment. At its simplest a string of outdoor lightbulbs slung overhead makes eating out a magical experience, but you can go further than that to get a theatrical effect: spotlights can be used to pinpoint a particular plant, floodlights to give a flood of light over a wall, or perhaps to highlight a statue. You can use underwater lights for a patio pool and, if you really want brightness after dark, tungsten lighting which can be fixed on a wall and directed on a flower bed where it will even make the weeds look a magical green! Use lighting to pinpoint just one area of the patio, the place you use for eating, then have just one spotlight elsewhere to point up some particular feature or use flares and candles, scattered strategically near interesting plants. (See also page 6.)

Eating out on the patio becomes still more fun if you cook out-of-doors as well, and it pays to think in terms of making your own barbecue. The simplest form of built-in barbecue is a rectangle of bricks lower in the front than the other three sides, onto which a metal grid is placed, with some sort of firebox below to hold the coals. If the barbecue is a low one, a layer of gravel on the surface of the terrace can be used as a base for the fire. But if you are making one at waist height, then a sheet of stout tin, sandwiched in between two courses of bricks will do. It's not necessary to buy a special barbecue kit; all sorts of kitchen items can be found that will do the job—from oven shelves to heavy duty cake racks. The two measurements to bear in mind are that the grill on which the food is cooked should ideally be about 15 inches/38 cm above the source of the fire to avoid scorching, and the grill itself must have gaps of no more than ½ inch/1 cm in it, or smaller items of food will fall through.

Given more space you can build the most elaborate looking barbecue area on the patio with surprising ease. A preparation area can be tacked on to one side of the barecue: another brick rectangle with a slab of marble off an old washstand set on top. And on the other side, if you have plenty of space, you could construct a smoker for making your own smoked fish and meat.

If you buy a factory-made barbecue instead, you have a choice between charcoal-burning models or those that work from bottled gas. In either case, it's important to have somewhere to stow the kit under cover when it is not in use; otherwise it will quickly deteriorate. The more elaborate barbecues can be extremely heavy; choose a model with wheels, rather than one that has to be dismantled, then carried and put away.

Statues and ornaments of all kinds are very much a matter of personal taste. Bear in mind one basic principal when buying: what looks good in a large garden centre might overwhelm a small patio, and in the case of statues in particular, avoid anything that is larger than life-size unless your area is very large. Here again, it pays to look around junk shops to find something unique. A slightly damaged wooden carving can sometimes be picked up cheaply; preserved against the worst of the weather, it would look good in a corner or against a wall. Or you could become an art patron; go to end of term shows at the local school of art, where you might find something interesting. Another unusual source for decorative figures is the trade exhibition; sometimes exhibitors have pieces of work made for display carved out of polystyrene. Believe it or not, this will last for years out-of-doors and acquires a respectable coating of algae in no time at all. One London garden contains a giant reclining Buddha which looks as though it is carved out of stone. Only when you touch it do you realise it is actually made out of foam plastic.

When a return to romantic gardening, arbours and bowers are coming back into fashion: rose-covered arches with seats underneath. An arbour is a good way of adding welcome shade in a hot, sunny corner. It can be constructed easily in several ways: a length of diamond trellis, for instance, can be bent into an arch with ease, then secured with the addition of strong battening on each edge. The seat inside might be an attractive small bench, or you could use a suitably sized stone trough, fill it with soil and plant chamomile or thyme on the top to form a natural, perfumed plant cushion—as the Elizabethans did in their gardens.

A full-sized swing, strong enough to take adults can make an attractive arbour if you grow roses up the framework—an idea this time from India. It takes up less space than the conventional swing settee and looks more attractive.

TEN CLIMBERS TO TRY

Clematis

Not just one climber of course but a whole family of climbing plants, all with exotic looking flowers, which are mainly deciduous. They do best in a sunny situation (though the large-flowered varieties can cope with shade) and like a cool root-run, i.e. shade around the base of the plant. Best bought as container-grown plants—since disturbing their roots while planting them may set them back—they can go into the ground any time during the winter months. Remember that the stems of young plant are fragile; treat them with care, especially when tying them up to a support.

Grape Vine (Vitis vinifera)

A very attractive climber to grow around the dining area on the patio, or against any sunny wall for the bonus of fruit. It can be trained to make an attractive overhead framework, with bunches of grapes dangling in the autumn. For sheer display, as well as attractive fruit, try V.vinifera "Brandt", a swift grower, which often produces attractive bunches of black grapes in its first year. The foliage turns golden-red in the autumn before the leaves drop. Once established, grape vines grow swiftly; but during the first year you may want to plant an annual climber to accompany them.

Honeysuckle (Lonicera)

Grown for its perfume as much as its flowers, this old-fashioned cottage climber is not too fussy about its situation. (choose Lonicera americana for really exposed or shaded walls). For scent, and for a stunning display all summer through, plant the early and late Dutch honeysuckles—L. belgica and L. serotina. If you want an evergreen climber, you will have to forego the perfume and choose the unscented L. brownii which usually keeps its leaves all the year. Lonicera natida, the true evergreen honeysuckle, is not a climber but a shrub, grown for its dense foliage, which is usually clipped into topiary shapes.

Hydrangea (Hydrangea petiolaris)

This climbing hydrangea looks quite unlike its shrubby cousin but has waxy, dark green leaves and more delicate white flowers. Its main claim to fame is that it can cope with shady walls and is a self-clinger, attaching itself to brickwork by adhesive pads. Difficult to get going—it may sulk for the first year—it is an excellent, permanent, almost evergreen plant which appreciates plenty of water.

Ivy (Hedera)

Most people think of ivy as a boring plant for walls, but it has many advantages. It gives an instant "antique" look to a newly built wall or fence, for instance, convincing you that it – and the wall – have been there a long time. It is also self-clinging and does not need tying up; it is of course also evergreen. Ivy has a bad reputation for damaging the walls it clings to, but if the mortar in the brickwork is sound, it can do no harm. Don't limit yourself to plain, dark green foliage; ivy comes in so many leaf sizes (from miniature to almost hand-sized) and so many variegations (splashed with gold, silver or white) that there are now specialist nurseries supplying just this one family of plants. Good on shady walls, easy to grow from cuttings, ivy will be encouraged to start climbing if you spray the wall with liquid manure. Remember that ivy can also be used successfully as ground cover, especially on raised beds.

Jasmine (Jasminum nudiflorum, officinale)

A pair of climbers that will give you colour both winter and summer. Jasminum nudiflorum produces starry yellow flowers in midwinter on bare branches and is technically a wall shrub rather than a climber. Jasminum officinale has fragrant white flowers and will keep its leaves on for most, but not all of the year. Both the jasmines can cope with shade.

Roses (Rosa)

If space is limited around the patio, a climbing rose may be the only variety you can choose, since shrub or hybrid tea roses take up a great deal of space and look unattractive when not in flower. Old-fashioned shrub roses are the most vigorous and are less likely to be prone to black spot and other diseases that strike more modern hybrids. Some climbers, notably Gloire de Dijon and Danse de Feu, are good for shaded walls. The yellow Mermaid is a good choice for a small space. Don't forget that there are now miniature climbing roses, too.

Russian Vine (Polygonum baldschuanicum)
If you're looking for something to smother a wall in a short time, this is the climber for you. It has long, oval green leaves, white racemes of flowers and is deciduous, leaving a dense tangle of brown stems in winter. Since it is also invasive, keep it under control—one way of doing so is to grow it in a large tub. In time the stems become gnarled and very like those of the grape vine. The Russian vine climbs by twirling stems but may need some tying at first. It can also be clipped to form a hedge against a wall.

Virginia Creeper (Parthenocissus quinquefolia)
This is another very useful climber, attaching itself to the wall without aid by suction pads on its tendrils. It is grown mainly for its spectacular autumn colouring which can look unpleasantly hot against red brick but wonderful against a whitewashed wall. The Virginia creeper does not like to have its roots disturbed, so buy it as a container-grown plant and put it into the ground with care. It may need to be staked until it has a proper hold on its host wall.

Wisteria (Wisteria sinensis)
Surely the most attractive of all climbers, with its lavender coloured trailing flowers, wisteria prefers a sunny site (though W. floribunda can take some shade) and may take a little while to start growing vigorously. Once under way, however, it can be trained into many different shapes including a weeping standard specimen tree. It needs a rich soil to do well.

SEVEN EVERGREEN TREES AND SHRUBS

Berberis

A good-tempered evergreen wall shrub that will reward you first of all with small yellow flowers and then with brilliant red-berries. In many varieties the leaves also turn purple red in autumn—B. aggregata and B. thunbergii, for instance. Keep berberis in mind if you are thinking of planting a hedge, for they make a fine, dense thicket.

Box (Buxus)

A good small evergreen that will suit any scale of patio since its leaves are tiny. Another similar, more slow-growing choice would be yew (Taxus). Box makes good edging or hedging but if grown as a single bush it is better clipped into a simple topiary shape—a pyramid or a cone—since it otherwise becomes rather straggly. It can take sunlight or shade, and any type of soil.

Camellia

A really handsome evergreen with its glossy dark green leaves and beautiful flowers. Camellias can take shade but should not be put in an exposed position where they get early morning sun on frosty flowers and frost burning will result. Camellias come with both double and single flowers; the williamsii cultivars are the sturdiest for a small garden. This shrub prefers an acid soil; if yours is not suitable, either grow it in a pot of specially made compost, or feed it regularly with chelate of iron.

False Cypress (Chamaecyparis lawsoniana)

A family of slow-growing conifers that make excellent hedges (if you clip off their growing tips), or specimen plants. Some of them have blue-green foliage, others, like Ellwood's Gold have yellow tips on the ends of their leaves. Elwoodii has a particularly attractive pyramid shape, and dense grey-green foliage. Conifers need plenty of water when they are first planted, or you may lose them.

Fatsia japonica

This shrub looks so exotic, with its large, glossy green leaves, that it is difficult to believe that it is hardy. Yet it is quite happy in the darkest corner of the patio. It can take city conditions well too. In autumn fatsia produces large white flowers very like giant dandelion clocks on stiff white stems. It will grow well in pots too.

Mexican Orange Blossom (Choisya ternata)

A really attractive evergreen that is grown mainly for its white, star-like scented flowers in late spring/early summer. It grows very well against a wall and, although it will take some shade, prefers the sun. It dislikes badly drained soils or heavy clay but is otherwise very tolerant.

Rhododendron

If you have an acid soil, or are willing to grow this shrub in a raised bed or pot of special compost, the rhododendron (and its smaller relative the azalea) makes a handsome shrub with colourful flowers from late spring to early summer. It is particularly good for a shallow bed since its roots tend to spread sideways rather than down; and it can be moved, if necessary, without its growth being checked. It is important to cover the top of the soil round it with a mulch of grass clippings, peat, or leaf-mould to retain the moisture because its roots are so near the surface. Keep an eye on it in times of drought, for it needs plenty of water. There are, incidentally, several small and dwarf varieties suitable for pots.

FIVE FLOWERING SHRUBS

Californian Lilac (Ceanothus)
Best suited to warm site—it is best grown against a
sheltered wall—this handsome evergreen has bright
blue flowers in early summer and averages 6–8 feet/
2–2.5 m in height when fully grown. It prefers a well
drained site and is not too happy with a chalky soil.
There is also a late-flowering version called autumnal
blue, which has darker blue flowers than the rest.

Deutzia
An obliging shrub that produces pink flowers that
look very much like dog roses in the case of some
hybrid versions, like white stars in others. Deutzias
can take almost any condition (except a very exposed
site) and are completely hardy. They are also at home
in shady woodland conditions.

Hydrangea
A much-maligned plant, probably because it is so
commonly seen, but an extremely useful one for it
grows particularly well in damp shade and is
therefore useful for dank corners. In addition to the
mop-headed hydrangeas, which are the best known,
there are lacecap hydrangeas which have flat heads
with tiny florets in the centre, the more usual petals
on the outside. Another version, H. paniculata has
pyramid-shaped flower heads. To get blue flowers
you must have an acid soil; alternatively, grow the
hydrangea in a pot and dose it with chelate of iron or
aluminium sulphate; your local garden centre probably sells a special mix for this purpose.

Olearia
Sometimes known as the "daisy bush" this shrub has
unremarkable leaves in a grey-green colouring but
dense numbers of daisy-like flowers with yellow
centres that make it very attractive in early summer.
It's available in pink or purple versions, too. Olearias
grow well by the sea; they like a medium-rich soil
and sunny site.

Skimmia japonica
A useful shrub which not only gives you creamy,
fragrant flowers in summer but bright red berries in
the early autumn. It makes a dense, well-rounded
bush, and the leaves are aromatic. Skimmia can take
sun or partial shade but prefer a more acid soil to one
with a large lime content.

PLANTS

PICKING PERENNIALS

There are so many perennial plants to choose from that it pays to have some sort of theme in mind when buying, all cottage garden flowers, for instance, perhaps based on daisy shapes; or a true mixed herbaceous border with spikes and clumps alternating.

Cottage garden flowers to look for include delphiniums (which need staking) and lupins, sweet Williams and stocks, Canterbury bells and marigolds. Michaelmas daisies and golden rod also go well in a mixed bed and now come in dwarf versions, which need less attention. Then of course there are flowers like London pride and forget-me-not.

Daisy-like flowers have an attractive simplicity about them that goes particularly well in pots. The shasta daisy (Chrysanthemum maximum) is a fast grower but may become invasive in time. Rudbeckias are easy to grow and come in sunshine yellows, while the real daisy Bellis perennis makes a pretty border.

Perennials need plenty of attention in the autumn if they are not to look untidy; dead and decaying stems and foliage should be removed during the winter months. From time to time the clumps will become too large; then split them. The easiest way to do this is to put two handforks back to back in the centre, and pull them apart. You may need to trim out the brown dead centre of the clump too, since all the new growth is around the outside.

GOING FOR GROUND COVER

If you have beds rather than pots to provide colour and interest around the patio, then you should certainly think of ground cover plants to cut down weeding, retain moisture, and at the same time provide another dimension of interest. The world of ground cover ranges from quite large plants like the St. John's wort (Hypericum), which is good on a large scale under shrubs in an island bed, to minute carpeters like mind-your-own-business (Helxine soleirolii) a tiny prostrate pink-stemmed plant which is good between paving stones.

Fragrance underfoot is another possibility since the prostrate form of Chamomile Anthemis nobilis (treneague) and the creeping thymes make marvellous ground cover and are tenacious once established. Pennyroyal with its strong minty scent is another possibility. Remember, too, that any climber can be pegged down to the soil to perform the same task.

Give ground cover plants a good start in life by planting them in clean soil. Alpines appreciate a little gravel mixed in for good drainage.

ANNUALS

Can easily be sown in tubs, window boxes and raised beds in early spring to give carpets of colour later on. If you want to beat the weather, however, sow them in soil blocks or peat pots indoors while the weather is still cool; then transfer them out-of-doors at seedling stage. Never place annuals in rows; the seed should be scattered in circles and crescents, preferably mixed. Packets of seed are still something of a bargain. Starting plants this way is often the only chance you have of trying the newer or more rare varieties. Plant a wildflower lawn in miniature for instance, in a corner bed, or enjoy the brief but beautiful colour of a tub full of poppies. If you can sow hardy annuals in late autumn, so much the better, for they will come up that much earlier and stronger next spring.

BEDDING PLANTS

Half-hardy specimens are what we rely on to give us the main colour around the patio. If you have the space and time, you can raise your own from seed indoors, but most of us buy them off a market barrow or at our local garden shop. The advantage of bedding plants is that they are instant: once set in place they burst into flower and continue to do so for weeks to come. The best bedding plants for shade are busy Lizzie (Impatiens) and begonias; while geraniums (Pelargonium) are sun-lovers. Fuchsia and petunias need plenty of water to keep them going, so keep an eye on them in high summer. Many bedding plants can winter over if you have space. As their growth dies down, cut down on the watering, bring them into a cool but frost-free place and start watering and feeding again when growth restarts.

Remember, too, that many houseplants can be set outside in mid-summer and used as bedding plants out-of-doors among them coleus with its brilliantly coloured leaves. All houseplants appreciate a spell on the patio when they can live, however briefly, in something nearer their natural condition.

MIMULUS
primuloides

MULUS
primuloides

SEDUM
Weihenstephaner Gold

THE SMALL SPACE GARDENER'S CALENDAR

Mid Winter Mainly armchair gardening this month: go through the catalogues and order seeds and the last of the shrubs. Work depends on the weather—it's still time to plant trees and shrubs if the weather is warm. Check anything that you have put into the ground to make sure the soil around it has not been lifted by hard frost. Lily bulbs can go into tubs for the patio.

Late Winter If you haven't divided up overly large clumps of perennials, do so before they spring into growth again. If you have snowdrops around the patio, they may need dividing up after they have flowered. Some shrubs may need pruning—outdoor fuchsia, buddleia, and clematis, for instance, which bloom in midsummer. If you have adequate indoor facilities, you can start sowing half-hardy items like petunias and geraniums for an early display.

Early Spring Everything depends now on the weather. Hybrid tea roses should be pruned before they burst their buds and—if the weather is fine—you can start planting out perennials. Seed of hardy annuals like sweet peas can go straight into the ground now. Plant bulbs of late-flowering lilies like Nerines too. If you have kept chrysanthemums and dahlias out for the winter, you can start growing cuttings from them.

Mid Spring Polyanthus and primulas that have flowered should be divided up now if they have formed large clumps. As the daffodils die down, take off their flowering heads but don't bend over and tie the leaves; this is a vital time for their work of sending food back down into the bulb ready for next year. Later when the leaves have completely died off, you can lift the bulbs if you wish. Shrubs like forsythia that have already flowered should be pruned back at this stage. And you can continue to sow hardy annual seed.

Late Spring Keep an eye on hardy annuals started from seed; they may need thinning out at this stage. And it's time to sow biennials like the wallflower (Cheiranthus) and the forget-me-not (Myosotis) for a display of flowers next year. Dahlias can go out now, and you can start to buy bedding flowers and plant hanging baskets, window boxes and troughs ready for a summer display. Don't put them out-of-doors until the end of the month, however, since late frosts are the most damaging of all.

Early Summer The hanging basket season is now at its height. Keep an eye on your baskets to make sure they have enough water to get properly established. If you have roses in the garden, spray them, as a precautionary measure, against mildew and black spot. Keep an eye open for aphids. As early flowering shrubs finish blooming, prune them back if necessary. Plant out autumn crocus bulbs for a late display. And if necessary, tie tall perennials to stakes to keep flower beds tidy.

Mid Summer This is the start of the watering season. From now on you may need to do hanging baskets twice a day. Dead-head your roses as they finish blooming to encourage a fresh wave of flowers. Cut sweet peas for the house to persuade

them to produce more blooms. This is the time to collect seeds from favourite flowers; choose a warm, dry day, when the early morning dew is off the plants, and pick off the seed heads carefully. Spread the seed to dry in a fairly cool indoor room; then put them in labelled paper envelopes and store in a cool dry drawer until next year. You can now start sowing perennials straight into the ground, ready for plants next year.

Late Summer The holiday season—and it will be necessary to find a "sitter" for your patio plants. If no help is forthcoming, move tubs and troughs into the shade, but still out of doors so that they get any rain that falls. Keep the patio tidy by dead-heading flowering plants the moment they have finished and raking up dead foliage. You can take cuttings of geraniums, fuchsia and other display plants; choose short, fat shoots rather than tall, spindly ones. Dip them in hormone rooting powder and place in a ring round the inner edge of the pot. Cover with a tent of clear plastic (a sandwich bag is fine) to keep the moisture in, and leave somewhere away from direct sunlight until the cuttings have taken. Continue to spray your roses to keep them free from disease, and wage a war against aphids.

Early Autumn Autumn comes all too soon in the patio garden, but try to extend the season by putting out a last wave of bedding plants. This is the time of course, for the chrysanthemums to take over. If you're planning a major planting programme, dig over beds as they become vacant, ready for the new incumbents. Start planting bulbs.

Mid Autumn Raking up time. Clear decaying vegetation; finish dead-heading flowers; pull up hardy annuals that have finished, but don't dig over the ground if you have left them to self-seed. This is bulb planting time, and tulips should go in during the last week of the month. Precious, less hardy trees and shrubs in tubs should be moved to a more sheltered position, if necessary, than that they have occupied all summer. Spring lily bulbs should go in now. Cut down perennials and tidy them up as they die off at the end of the season. Bring half-hardy plants indoors.

Late Autumn Finish planting spring bulbs and put in trees and shrubs that you ordered earlier, before the ground freezes hard. You can also put in herbaceous plants at this stage. Try your luck with some hardwood cuttings; take sprigs of winter jasmine and buddleia and push them in the ground in an odd corner—some of them will take, and you'll have a supply of free shrubs that way.

Early Winter Keep an eye on the weather charts; if severe frost is forecast, wrap up tubs containing trees and shrubs, with sacking or even newspaper tied around the outside. Roots of these plants are far less protected in pots than they are in the ground, and you could lose some specimens. If sharp frosts strike, take a look at anything you planted in the autumn to make sure that the soil has not cracked and lifted around them, thus letting in the cold. Finally settle back and send for those seed catalogues.

INDEX